**Donated by the
Friends of the Library**

MARKUS
ZUSAK

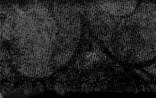

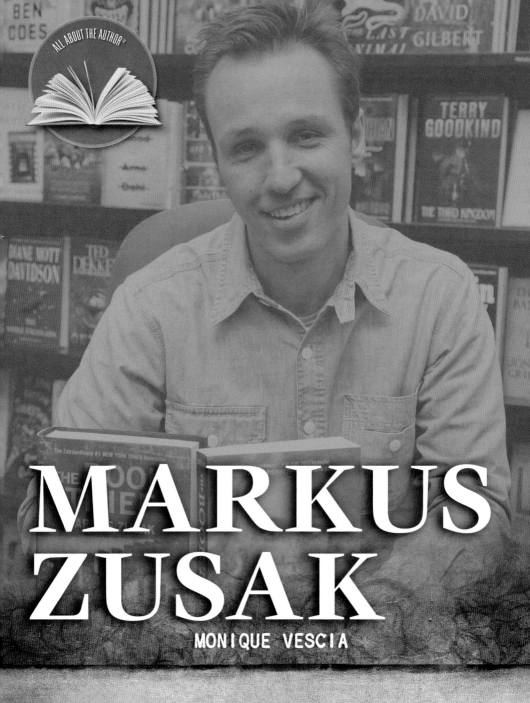

MARKUS ZUSAK

MONIQUE VESCIA

ROSEN
PUBLISHING®

New York

Published in 2015 by The Rosen Publishing Group, Inc.
29 East 21st Street, New York, NY 10010

First Edition

Library of Congress Cataloging-in-Publication Data

Vescia, Monique.
Markus Zusak/Monique Vescia.—First Edition.
    pages cm.—(All About the Author)
Includes bibliographical references.
ISBN 978-1-4777-7908-8 (library bound)
1. Zusak, Markus—Juvenile literature. 2. Authors, Australian—Biography—Juvenile
literature. 3. Young adult fiction—Authorship—Juvenile literature. I. Title.
PR9619.4.Z87Z93 2015
823'.92—dc23
[B]

                                                                    2014016863

Manufactured in China

CONTENTS

INTRODUCTION 6

CHAPTER ONE   AROUND THE KITCHEN TABLE........ 9

CHAPTER TWO   LIFE IN OZ: GROWING UP
                  DOWN UNDER 20

CHAPTER THREE   "MAKE FAILURE YOUR FRIEND":
                  THE *UNDERDOGS* TRILOGY.................. 28

CHAPTER FOUR   THE WRITER'S TASKS: *THE MESSENGER*...... 38

CHAPTER FIVE   STEALING STORIES: THE GENESIS
                  OF *THE BOOK THIEF* 46

CHAPTER SIX   THE RUNAWAY SUCCESS OF *THE BOOK THIEF*... 57

CHAPTER SEVEN   COURAGE BEYOND WORDS: THE MAKING
                  OF *THE BOOK THIEF* MOVIE................. 66

CHAPTER EIGHT   TURNING THE PAGE: *BRIDGE OF CLAY*...... 78

                  FACT SHEET ON MARKUS ZUSAK 84

                  FACT SHEET ON MARKUS ZUSAK'S WORKS .. 86

                  CRITICAL REVIEWS.................... 89

                  TIMELINE........................ 91

                  GLOSSARY........................ 94

                  FOR MORE INFORMATION........ 97

                  FOR FURTHER READING 102

                  BIBLIOGRAPHY........... 104

                  INDEX............... 108

Markus Zusak (pronounced ZOO-zack) might have an unusual-sounding name, but today it is a name known around the world. Early in his career as a writer, there were times when he was scheduled to speak, and not a single person showed up to hear him read from his books. Now, his public appearances draw huge crowds, who hang on Zusak's every word. One of the most successful writers ever to hail from Australia, he autographs copies of his books—and sometimes even doodles on the front pages—hundreds of times per sitting.

When Zusak talks about his craft, he stresses the importance of failure in his evolution as a writer. He feels grateful that publishers rejected his early manuscripts because it forced him to recognize that he needed to improve. On his Facebook page, Zusak introduces himself as a "Writer, mistake-maker, and fan of *Sam-I-Am*...I wrote *The Book Thief*, but still not sure how."

This Dr. Seuss fan and Sydney native, who almost always writes in the first person (though not the same person), first drew upon his own experiences for a trilogy of compelling tales about a pair of working-class Australian brothers. A fifteen-minute parking zone gave him the idea for his next novel, which had mystery and humor and a dog named The Doorman. But Zusak found his greatest success when he chose to channel the voice of Death to tell the story of a

Markus Zusak drew on his parents' stories of World War II to craft a best-selling book that eventually became a movie. He still seems amazed by his own success.

ten-year-old German girl confronting the horrors of the Holocaust, fighting words with words.

Zusak has dark hair and eyes, straight white teeth, and a boxer's nose. Thanks to his talent, youth, and relaxed charm—and maybe his Aussie accent—Zusak has amassed a large following of avid admirers all over the world. They create fan pages in his honor, where they post photographs of the author and quotes from his books; they share videos of his talks and quiz one another on their knowledge of his works.

All of this is still new enough to Zusak that he finds it hard to sleep after a book reading; he feels all jazzed up, the adrenaline still coursing through him. Clearly, he has made an effort to avoid allowing this adulation to go to his head. In interviews, Zusak is funny and self-effacing. His responses to fans' messages and questions are always measured, thoughtful, and polite. And when he wants to make a point or explain something about his process as a writer, Zusak does what he does best: he tells a story.

AROUND THE KITCHEN TABLE

Markus Frank Zusak was born on June 23, 1975, in Sydney, New South Wales, Australia. The youngest of four children in a rough-and-tumble household, Markus came into the world in the middle of winter in the Southern Hemisphere. He was born into a working-class family, a child of immigrant parents; his father made his living as a house painter, and Markus's mother cleaned houses to help support the family. With his two German-speaking parents, Markus grew up hearing that language at home.

WAR STORIES

People often say that the kitchen is the heart of any house. The warmth of the stove and the smells of cooking often draw people to gather there. This adage

was especially true in the Zusak household. Little Markus, along with his older brother and their two sisters, often clustered around the kitchen table, where their parents enthralled them with stories of their experiences during World War II. His mother, Elizabeth, grew up in a village outside Munich, the city in southern Germany where Adolf Hitler's National Socialist (Nazi) Party originated. Allied bombing raids leveled Munich at the end of the war, and the bombs, of course, did not discriminate between Nazi supporters and German civilians who rejected Hitler's doctrine of hate. Elizabeth, who went by "Lisa" but was nicknamed "Liesel" as a child, had vivid memories of the cruelty of war and the destruction of her home city. A gifted storyteller, she captivated her children with

riveting tales of life in Germany during wartime. During the mid-1950s, when Lisa was twenty-one,

In May 1945, homeless Germans cook food in open ovens in the bomb-damaged city of Nuremberg, once host to Nazi Party festivals and later the site of the famous war trials.

she decided to immigrate to the Australian state of New South Wales. There, she met and fell in love with an Austrian man named Helmut, who lived right next door.

SYDNEY: A CITY OF IMMIGRANTS

Situated around a beautiful natural harbor on the southeast coast of Australia and crowned by the striking architecture of its famous opera house, Sydney boasts an array of cultures and communities.

The world's largest steel arch bridge, the Sydney Harbour Bridge, is a much-photographed landmark in the state capital city of Sydney, where locals call it "the Coathanger."

But this thriving metropolis, the most populous city in Australia, actually began as a British penal colony. Starting in 1788, prisoners were sent there from Great Britain. British and Irish immigrants followed in the 1830s and 1840s.

As in the United States, immigrants came to Sydney for various reasons, some seeking better opportunities and others fleeing persecution or wars in their home countries. Some came illegally or unwillingly, others by choice. As in the American West, Australia experienced its own gold rushes during the mid-nineteenth century. Thousands of Chinese immigrants came to labor in the gold fields.

Between 1945 and 1965, more than two million immigrants came to Australia. Markus's parents were among them. By 2010, 27 percent of Australians were born overseas and more than one hundred different languages were spoken.

Helmut Zusak, Markus's father, had his own war stories, though he couldn't quite match his wife's talent for storytelling. Helmut grew up in Vienna, Austria, a beautiful city and vibrant cultural center. When the German army invaded Austria in the spring of 1938, it met with no resistance. In some cases, crowds turned out to welcome the soldiers as they marched down Vienna's main streets. As Markus listened to his parents' tales of those times, images from their stories took root in the young boy's imagination.

FRANK, THE ANKLE-BITER

When Markus was a little kid, or an "ankle-biter," as they say in Strine (Australian English slang), he hated his first name. He preferred to go by his middle name, Frank, and wanted no one to call him Markus. As the youngest of four children, he often felt cheated out of activities that his siblings enjoyed, such as horseback riding, because he was too little to participate. His position in the family order made him fiercely ambitious because he often felt he had gotten the short end of the stick. He loved Froot Loops cereal, but his parents only let the kids eat this as a treat during the summer, and they all fought over the plastic toy prize in the box. Markus's embattled relationship with his older brother, in particular, eventually would become the inspiration for his first published novel and the sequels that followed.

GRUG AND THE SAUSAGE-ROLL THIEF

His parents' stories weren't the only tales that fascinated Markus as a child. Perhaps it's not surprising that he would go on to become a writer—his mother remembers that as a child Markus was always immersed in a book. Among his favorites were those

HOW TO SPEAK STRINE: A GLOSSARY OF AUSTRALIAN SLANG

ankle-biter: A small child.
drongo: An unintelligent and worthless person.
earbash: To talk nonstop.
make a crust: To work for a living.
mate: A term that can refer to a man or a woman.
Never-never, or Outback: The most remote parts of the Australian bush.
oldies: Parents.
Oz: A name for Australia.
shark biscuit: An inexperienced surfer.
stickybeak: A nosy person.
Strine: Australian slang.
tucker: Food.

featuring Grug, the star of a popular series of children's books by Australian author Ted Prior. Grug, who began his life at the top of a burrawang tree, looks like a small striped haystack with a face. In books such as *Grug and the Red Apple*, Grug is fascinated by the world around him and frequently finds creative ways to solve problems. In one story, Grug has trouble following some dancing instructions, so he invents his own dance called "The Grug."

15

Australian children are familiar with the burrawang tree, an Aboriginal name for a cycad with highly poisonous seeds, where the freewheeling fictional character Grug was born.

Markus sometimes found his own way to solve problems, too. When he was hungry at school one day, he stole a sausage roll from the school canteen. Much to his disappointment, it was still frozen.

FROM PAINTBRUSH TO PEN

The first thing Markus wanted to be was a footballer (soccer player). That dream died as soon as he faced the facts that he wasn't physically big enough or good enough, and he really hated training. His father made his living as a house painter. Early on, Markus thought he might like to follow in his dad's footsteps, so he accompanied his father on some of his jobs to get a feel for the work. Markus was just ten the first time he went

Markus's father, Helmut, made his living as a house painter, but Markus had no affinity for the work. He imagined a different career for himself—one as a storyteller.

with his father on a painting job. He was the right size to crawl into a small space for storing luggage, and to paint the inside. He ended up painting himself into a corner and had to wait an hour for the paint to dry before he could crawl out. After making a lot of mistakes, such as spilling paint and tracking mud into houses, Markus realized he had no talent for house painting. He also found the work extremely boring.

Around this time, Markus made a crucial discovery, one that would change the course of his life. He realized that, as a result of his parents' stories, an entirely different world existed inside his head. If he could become a writer and tell stories of his own, he could perform the same kind of magic.

TWO

LIFE IN OZ: GROWING UP DOWN UNDER

Markus grew up in the southern suburbs of Sydney, known to locals as the Sutherland Shire. The Shire is a homogenous area, populated largely by British-Irish Australians. Markus attended Engadine High School in Sydney. Markus's brother, who was two years ahead of him in school, would often punch his younger brother as he passed by or drag him down the hall so that Markus would be late for his next class.

A SYDNEYSIDER TEEN

When they returned home from school each day, the brothers had a friendlier ritual: they made themselves some toast and sat down to watch *Get Smart*, an old television comedy series about a bumbling secret agent.

Sydneysiders, as Sydney residents call themselves, know that their hometown ranks as one of the world's best surfing cities. When he wasn't studying for school or working on his writing, Markus could often be found riding his board through the waves at Manly or Bondi Beach. In an April 2006 interview in *Teenreads*, Markus said,

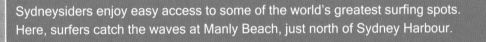

Sydneysiders enjoy easy access to some of the world's greatest surfing spots. Here, surfers catch the waves at Manly Beach, just north of Sydney Harbour.

"One of my best memories of growing up is catching my first proper wave, surfing across it, with my brother cheering from the shore. My brother and I hated each other and loved each other, but that small memory shows me that we were really best friends." Memories like these would become part of the material for his first successes as a writer.

WRITE WHAT YOU KNOW

Aspiring authors are often encouraged to mine their own personal experiences for material and story ideas. Writing teachers counsel their students to "write what you know," to find their authentic voices. Markus's first successful works (that is, the ones that got published) were based on a subject close to his heart: his relationship with his older brother. Brothers can be both competitive and supportive; they seek each other's approval at the same time that they battle for their parents' attention. Markus's relationship with his own brother provided the model for his fictional Wolfe brothers' relationship, which he explored in the triad of novels now published together as *Underdogs*. As Zusak wrote in his 2010 foreword to the collection, "Cameron and Ruben Wolfe were a pair of boys I knew without question. The voice of Cameron was me. The spirit of Ruben was my brother."

THE BENEFITS OF SOLITUDE

Markus also has described himself as kind of a loner when he was a teenager. He was a kid who spent a lot of time with his nose buried in a book. When he read or watched movies, he identified with the characters on the fringes of the action rather than

READING TO WRITE

Reading is an essential practice in a writer's development. Writers hone their craft by writing, but they also learn by studying the works of other writers. As the novelist W. P. Kinsella once advised, "Read! Read! Read! And then read some more. When you find something that thrills you, take it apart paragraph by paragraph, line by line, word by word, to see what made it so wonderful. Then use those tricks the next time you write." Markus's decision to become a writer stemmed from his love of books. He wanted to create the kind of magic that he experienced as a reader transported into the world of a story. Because they were not native English speakers, the Zusaks made sure that their home was full of books in English for their children to read. Two books that inspired Markus in his writing efforts were Ernest Hemingway's *The Old Man and the Sea* and Peter Hedges's *What's Eating Gilbert Grape*.

those in the spotlight. Finding time to oneself while growing up in a big and boisterous family can be a challenge. Writing is a solitary craft, and many writers enjoy spending time alone. Markus used whatever time he had alone to develop his skills as a storyteller.

FIRST DRAFTS

When he was sixteen, Markus decided he would write a novel. He thought he had a fantastic story to tell, about a boy who had a cyst in his head that could blow up at any moment. Unfortunately (or maybe not!), he only made it to page eight before he ran out of steam and abandoned the project. In the classroom, he was much better at writing essays than he was at creative writing. All in all, he was not a top student in his English classes.

Markus's early failures turned out to be important to his development as a writer. Rather than feeling discouraged, Markus realized he needed to become a better writer, and he kept trying. As the young-est child, he had learned how to fight for what he wanted. He was determined and would not give up.

COLLEGE DAYS

When Markus enrolled in college at the University of New South Wales, he had a pretty clear idea where his interests lay. He chose to major in history and

Zusak attended the University of New South Wales in his home city of Sydney. That institution has produced more millionaires than any university in Australia.

English, two subjects that seemed natural choices, given his love of storytelling. He knew he wanted to be an author, but he also had to think practically. What could he do to earn a living if his books didn't sell? He already knew a thing or two about rejection, and though he was committed to perfecting his craft, writing was never easy for him—he always struggled to produce something that satisfied him. Teaching seemed a logical choice, so he set out to earn a teaching degree.

BACK TO THE BEGINNING

Once he had his degree in hand, Zusak ended up right back where he'd started: teaching English literature classes at his alma mater, Engadine High School. He told the *Sydney Morning Herald*, "I liked being with teenagers, but I was just really bad at telling them what to do." He did not consider himself a very good teacher. Jade Catton, one of his former students, would disagree. Catton wrote that Zusak

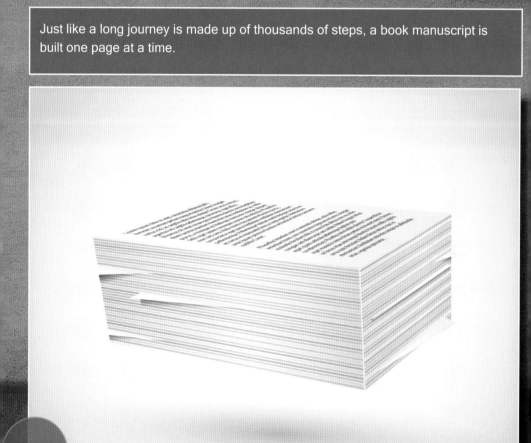

Just like a long journey is made up of thousands of steps, a book manuscript is built one page at a time.

was "as great a person/teacher as he is a writer. My favourite memory of him was his decision to paint the classroom (without permission) with scenes from Bob Dylan's song 'Hurricane' which we were studying at the time. Needless to say he got into huge trouble and had to repaint the room back to its original colour!" Zusak also ended up working part time as a janitor after he graduated from college and doing some tutoring, as well.

NEVER GIVE UP

Zusak was writing all the time, but he couldn't finish anything. Nonetheless, he kept at it, and ultimately that perseverance paid off. As he said to the *Sydney Morning Herald*, "If you keep showing up at your desk, then you know you're a writer." But if he expected to make a living at this kind of work, he needed an audience. Eventually, it would take him seven long years of repeated rejections before one of his manuscripts was finally accepted for publication.

THREE

"MAKE FAILURE YOUR FRIEND": THE *UNDERDOGS* TRILOGY

Markus Zusak's career as a published writer began with a nightmare trip to the dentist, some expensive and painful dental work, and dreams of revenge. He asked himself: what if two brothers tried to rob a dentist? And what if they came armed with a baseball bat and a cricket bat? And what if they were so captivated by the dentist's beautiful receptionist that they ended up getting checkups instead?

Though he claims that appearing in front of audiences raises his heart rate and gets his adrenaline surging, Zusak looks quite relaxed at this book-signing event.

THE ORIGINS OF
THE UNDERDOG

When Zusak started to write *The Underdog*, he thought it would be a short story. But the subject matter—a tale of two hapless, battling brothers—was something he knew by heart and which just seemed to flow out of him. As he states in the foreword to the *Underdogs* trilogy, he had a great time

A WRITER'S ROUTINE

Many novelists work from a home office. In that environment, with the telephone and television close by and family members poking their heads around the door to ask, "When's dinner?" it can be a real challenge to focus. Writers often find that having a regular routine helps minimize distractions and makes them more productive. Zusak's writing habit is to be at his desk by 7:00 every morning and to work until around 11:30 AM, when he takes a long break. Then he's back at his desk for a few more hours of work. (Zusak's dog, Reuben, has a similar routine, except he's under the desk.) When he's finishing up a book, Zusak will put in longer hours. In summer (that's from December to February in Australia), he usually goes surfing in the early mornings and doesn't get to his desk until closer to 10:00.

writing what quickly turned into a novel, just playing with words "like a kid in a sandpit." *The Underdog* took Zusak just a few months to write and edit.

FAIL, FAIL, FAIL AGAIN

During the previous seven years, Zusak had submitted three other manuscripts to publishers. Every one had been turned down. He fully expected that *The Underdog* would be rejected, too—after all, he had worked much harder on the other three books. Still, he wrapped it up to send out to publishers. Around this time, he had plans to take his first trip overseas. What happened next is a story in itself, one that illustrates the kind of relationship the author had with his brother. In the forward to the *Underdogs* trilogy, he wrote, "I left the manuscript under my bed with fifty dollars attached, for my brother to mail for me while I was away. When I rang to ask him to send it off, he did what any self-respecting older brother would do. He paid the eight dollars to mail it and kept the forty-two dollars change."

Zusak had embarked on his travels, fully expecting to return home to find another rejection letter in the mailbox.

AN UNEXPECTED PHONE CALL

Zusak was staying in Vienna with his dad's best friend when the phone rang at about two o'clock in the morning. Usually a phone call in the middle of the night brings bad news, but Zusak says that when he heard the ringing, he just knew: his father was calling to tell him the publisher had accepted his book. When Zusak called to share the exciting news with his siblings, his sisters jumped for joy but, in typical fashion, his brother only said, "Pretty good." Markus knew, from his brother, this was the equivalent of high praise.

A SYDNEYSIDER ROMANCE

This 1998 trip, Zusak's first to Germany and Austria, proved memorable for another reason: it was during his travels that he met his future wife. Ironically, he had to travel thousands of miles to find someone who came from his own hometown. Dominika is a fellow Sydneysider from a Polish family. She and Zusak traveled together for a while in Europe, then met up again in Sydney. The couple was married in 2000. Dominika has a business background, and she and Markus share the household work. They have two children, a girl and a boy.

THE FIRST OF THREE

Zusak's first novel, *The Underdog*, came out in 1999 in Australia when he was twenty-four. He drew deeply upon his own experiences to write the story about two Australian brothers. The novel plays with the idea that boys are like dogs, "ready to bite, bark, and beg to be given a chance to show their value." Cameron Wolfe, the fifteen-year-old protagonist and narrator of the story, and his older brother, Ruben, are always getting into fights, cooking up crazy schemes to make money, and annoying the other Wolfe family members. Cameron, a loner with a big heart, lives in Ruben's shadow, dreams about finding a girlfriend, and worries about his dad's job and his blue-collar family's well-being.

Once he succeeded in publishing his fourth attempt at a novel, Zusak found he was able to "make a crust," or (just barely) support himself as a writer. He traveled around the country to different schools, where he was paid to talk about his writing. On one memorable gig, Zusak drove eleven hours through the night to get to a school where he was scheduled to speak. The crows on the lawn outside cawed loudly during his whole talk.

RETURN OF THE WOLFE BROTHERS

The Underdog turned out to be just the first installment of what would become a trilogy. Zusak's second book about the Wolfe clan,

Fighting Ruben Wolfe (2000), was published a year later. In the follow-up novel, the brothers begin boxing for money after their father loses his job. *Kirkus Reviews* described the book as

ADVICE FOR ASPIRING WRITERS

In interviews, Zusak often mentions how grateful he is that publishers rejected his early manuscripts. Each time they turned down one of his submissions, he was forced to make efforts to improve his writing. Zusak believes that authors who publish too early in their careers might miss the opportunity to continue developing their craft. Rather than feeling discouraged and throwing in the towel, Zusak kept at it. He's convinced that his failures helped to make him a better writer.

To improve, a writer has to write. Zusak points out that you don't become a better runner by thinking about running—you have to go out and run. Sometimes, when the writing flows, working with words can feel like playing, but more often it's a struggle to express oneself. Even now that Zusak has written a best-selling novel and won a boatload of awards, he says it doesn't get any easier. He compares the writing process to climbing a mountain: it takes a huge amount of effort, but you feel incredible when you finally reach the summit.

"an intense tale of boxing, brotherly solidarity, and searching for self-respect." With each book he wrote, Zusak learned more about how to construct a good story on the page. Readers responded to his gritty characters and the eccentric, often poetic nature of his writing, but some reviewers complained about inconsistencies in the work.

In 2001, Zusak received a true honor: the Children's Book Council of Australia (CBCA) awarded *Fighting Ruben Wolfe* a Book of the Year Award for Older Readers. That same year, the novel was also shortlisted for the Ethel Turner Prize for Young People's Literature. Recognition like this is a big deal for writers, and for publishers, especially because listing such honors prominently on the front of dust jackets helps to sell books. Zusak's work was definitely attracting attention, and his career as a writer had begun to take off—in his home country of Australia and beyond.

THE LAST CHAPTER: *WHEN DOGS CRY*

The third and final book in the Wolfe brothers trilogy came out in 2002, delighting readers familiar with the first two books in the series. Aspiring

Self-promotion is part of a writer's job: Zusak travels to many cities and venues, including the *Guardian* Hay Festival in Wales, where he spoke in 2009.

writer Cameron Wolfe develops a crush on his brother's former girlfriend, Octavia, and in the course of the novel he finally emerges from Ruben's shadow. *When Dogs Cry* is also the title of one of Cameron's poems, which are interspersed throughout the novel. Zusak's American publishers might have thought the book's original title, *When Dogs Cry*, was too strange. In the U.S., the novel was published under the more straightforward title, *Getting the Girl*. In 2011, the entire trilogy would be reissued inside a single cover, called an "omnibus," titled *Underdogs*.

CHAPTER FOUR

THE WRITER'S TASKS: *THE MESSENGER*

nspiration for a story can strike a writer at any moment. According to his Random House profile, Zusak got the idea for his novel *The Messenger* when he was sitting in a park one night eating fish and chips with his wife: "[I] saw a bank with a fifteen-minute parking zone out the front, and I thought, 'Fifteen minutes, that's not very long—every time I go [to] the bank it takes a lot longer than that.' I then thought, 'What if you were in that bank when it was being robbed and your car was out in the fifteen-minute parking zone? How would you get out to move your car to avoid getting a fine?' That gave me the bungled bank robbery scene that led to everything else in the book."

An idea for a great story might turn up anywhere, even on a local parking sign. Good writers keep their eyes and ears open for unexpected sources of inspiration.

Published in 2002, *The Messenger* tells the story of nineteen-year-old Ed Kennedy, a hapless cab driver who can't seem to catch a break, and his coffee-drinking dog named The Doorman. But Ed's luck begins to change after he inadvertently foils a bank robbery and becomes a local hero. Soon after, he mysteriously receives a playing card in the mail— an ace of diamonds with three addresses and times written on it, representing a series of tasks that Ed must complete. More aces follow, with cryptic clues that Ed has to decode.

HONING HIS CRAFT

Readers and critics responded enthusiastically to the novel's blend of rough humor and suspenseful storytelling. *The Messenger* (retitled *I Am the Messenger* for publication in the United States) earned praise in highly regarded periodicals such as *School Library Journal*, *Booklist*, and *Kirkus Reviews*, garnering reviews that publishers featured prominently on reprints of the book. Practice was definitely paying off for the twenty-seven-year-old author. Zusak's writing became more self-assured with every novel that he published, and a growing number of readers were following this new writer's career with keen interest. A starred review in *Publishers Weekly* remarked on the elevation of his writing: "Zusak takes the subtleties of family dynamics, previously examined in his *Fighting Ruben Wolfe* and *Getting the Girl*, to a new level here."

A BOATLOAD OF AWARDS

This book, which had been sparked in Zusak's brain as he sat munching fish and chips in a park, would go on to win numerous awards. *The Messenger* won the 2003 Australian Children's Book Award: Older Readers, the same honor Zusak had received for *Fighting Ruben Wolfe*. In 2003, Zusak also took home Australia's Ethel Turner Prize for Young

People's Literature (and the $30,000 prize that comes with it) as well as the Children's Book Council Book of the Year Award (for Older Readers). In the United States, the novel scored a 2006 Michael L. Printz Honor Book Award. Across Europe, the novel earned many international readers' choice awards, including Germany's prestigious Deutscher Jugendliteratur ("German Youth Literature") prize.

A few years later, *The Messenger* was adapted by author Ross Mueller into a one-act play. Debuting at the Canberra Youth Theatre on November 26, 2008, the play received rave reviews; the Chief Minister ACT (Australian Capital Territory) declared that "[T]his is youth theatre at its best. The production is engaging, stimulating and skillfully tackles issues of importance not just to young people, but to our community as a whole."

THE PEOPLE BEHIND THE PRIZES

Book awards often bear the names of individuals with whom most readers are unfamiliar, so here's a bit of background on the people behind the prizes that Markus Zusak's books have won:

(continued on the next page)

(continued from the previous page)

Literacy advocate Margaret A. Edwards, who has a literary prize named in her honor, is shown distributing books to young people from an early type of bookmobile in Baltimore, Maryland, 1944.

Margaret A. Edwards (1902–1988): As administrator of young adult programs at the Enoch Pratt Free Library in Baltimore, Maryland, for more than thirty years, Margaret A. Edwards spent her life bringing books and young people together. Edwards pioneered outreach services for teenagers and established a training program designed especially for librarians beginning their work with adolescents. The award bearing her name recognizes a body of work that makes a significant and lasting contribution to young adult literature.

Michael L. Printz (1937–1996): Mike Printz was a beloved writer, teacher, and school librarian at Topeka West High School in Kansas. Before he died at age fifty-nine, he initiated an author-in-residence program at the high school and an oral history project for the state of Kansas. He was also infamous for playing practical jokes on his friends. The Michael L. Printz Award and up to four Michael L. Printz Award Honor Book prizes are given annually to the books that exemplify literary excellence in young adult literature.

Ethel Turner (1873–1958): One of Australia's best-loved authors, this novelist and writer of children's literature was born in England but grew up in Australia. Her book *Seven Little Australians* (1894), featuring the Woolcots, a fictional family of seven rambunctious children, was a huge hit in Australia and overseas. The Ethel Turner Prize is awarded for fiction, nonfiction, or poetry written for young people at the secondary school level.

CAN YOU TOP THIS?

Perhaps Zusak wondered, as he basked in the glow of all these honors, if he had reached the summit of his particular mountain. He had crafted a successful career for himself as a writer. He had become a highly respected and award-winning author, not only in his home country, but abroad, as well. His latest book had even been adapted into a successful stage play. How could he top these accomplishments?

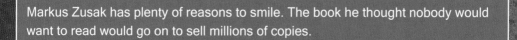

Markus Zusak has plenty of reasons to smile. The book he thought nobody would want to read would go on to sell millions of copies.

A NEW POINT OF VIEW

The first four books Zusak published had something in common: each was narrated by a young man who resembled the author himself. Zusak had taken the edict to "write what you know" to heart, and it had helped to launch his career. Beginning with the saga of the Wolfe brothers, which drew heavily on Zusak's own experiences growing up in the shadow of his own older brother, and moving on to the character of Ed Kennedy in *The Messenger*, Zusak's protagonists are young, Australian, working-class men who see themselves as failures. They crave love and scrape along to get by in the world, always fighting for some measure of self-respect. Zusak knew how to tell their stories, and he told them very well. For his next book, he had something else in mind, something entirely different.

CHAPTER FIVE

STEALING STORIES: THE GENESIS OF *THE BOOK THIEF*

Zusak's mother was born in Munich, Germany, and at the age of three was taken in by a foster family. As she liked to say, "I was born on a Sunday, christened on a Monday, fostered on a Tuesday," according to the *Sydney Morning Herald*. When Markus was a little boy, transfixed by his mother's tales about World War II, two stories in particular captured his imagination. He never forgot his mother's description of the sky burning and bombs falling on the houses across the road from where she lived. A little girl and her grandmother were killed in the raid.

This aerial photograph taken from a U.S. B-52 bomber records a strike on a German rubber factory during World War II.

Another time during the war, when Markus's mother was six years old, she heard what sounded like cattle coming down the street. When she looked outside she saw a group of Jewish prisoners being herded roughly along by Nazi soldiers. A teenage boy who lived next door saw them, too, and was moved to action by the sight of such misery. He ran from the house to bring a piece of bread to one of the starving prisoners. The prisoner wept in gratitude, thanking the boy. Then a soldier knocked the bread from the man's hands and viciously whipped the boy for his compassion.

CRUELTY AND COURAGE

For Zusak, this last image seemed incredibly power-ful. It captured people at their very worst, capable of terrible violence and cruelty, and at their very best, capable of selfless acts of deep compassion. As he later reflected in his Macmillan Publishers profile, "This showed me that there was another side to Nazi Germany, and it was a side I wanted to write about. At first I thought of a biography, but as a writer of fiction, I knew it wouldn't take long for the itch to imagine to climb out of me and into the story."

FROM NOVELLA TO NOVEL

When Zusak began writing *The Book Thief*, he imagined it would be a one-hundred-page novella about a German girl who steals books and reads them with a young Jewish man hiding in her family's basement. He named his main character Liesel, his mother's childhood nickname. Like his mother, Liesel is a foster child. Zusak has said that half of writing a book is forgetting that a world exists beyond that book. Before long, the story took hold of him and spirited him away. By the time Zusak was finished, his novella had grown into a 580-page book.

Every writer has a different working process, which might change from one book to the next. Zusak says that he generally has the beginning and end in place first. As he writes, he has certain "check points" he wants to hit, like a runner in a race. Zusak organized *The Book Thief* by listing chapter titles in a notebook and playing around with their order. The action of the novel is built out of short episodes and features many asides to the reader.

DEATH TELLS THE TALE

It took Zusak three years to write *The Book Thief*. During that time, his parents kept asking him when the book was going to be finished. He had some trouble figuring out who should narrate the story. For a while, he thought that Liesel Meminger, his protagonist, should be the narrator, but, as he wrote in a Tumblr blog post, she was "the most Australian-sounding German girl in the history of all books everywhere." As he worked through these and other problems, Zusak continued to learn from his missteps: "In three years, I must have failed over a thousand times, but each failure brought me closer to what I needed to write, and for that, I'm grateful," he says.

Zusak knew that many books had already been written about Nazi Germany. What could he do that was different and original, to make his story stand out from the rest? "Then I stumbled upon the idea of Death narrating the story, and it all made sense. Who is constantly hanging around in times of war? Who would have the opportunity to pick up a story penned by a girl in a bombed German city? Death was the right answer, although there were still a few decisions to be made."

At first, the voice of Death was very sadistic and seemed to find pleasure in describing terrible events. After two hundred pages, Zusak realized that wasn't the right tone for his story. Then, he hit upon the idea of making Death afraid of humans because of all the cruelty they inflict on one another. "He tells Liesel's story to remind him that humans can be beautiful and selfless and worthwhile," he blogged on Tumblr. Once Zusak came to the realization that

DON'T FEAR THE REAPER: DEATH PERSONIFIED

Throughout history, in mythology and art, humans have personified death. Death has been imagined as a skeletal figure wielding a huge scythe, an avenging angel, and a seductive woman, among other forms. Giving death human attributes makes an abstract and frightening concept seem less terrifying.

Markus Zusak put a new spin on this idea when he decided that Death, who narrates his story, should be haunted by humans, instead of the other way around. This brainstorm was key to the success of *The Book Thief*. Other prose works in which death assumes a human form include:

- **Edgar Allan Poe's 1842 story, "The Masque of the Red Death"**

- *The Tales of Beedle the Bard* **by J. K. Rowling**

- *A Dirty Job* **by Christopher Moore**

- **The** *Discworld* **graphic novel series by Terry Pratchett**

- **The** *Sandman* **graphic novel series by Neil Gaiman**

- *On a Pale Horse* **by Piers Anthony**

this was the right approach, he started the book all over again.

In its final form, the novel is very visual. Colors feature prominently in the story. Zusak incorporated sections in bold text, as well as pictures and diagrams in the narrative because he wanted to show that Death experiences the world in a slightly different way from human beings. This difference is also expressed in the way that Death personalizes inanimate things such as the sky. In one instance, Death refers to "the blinding, white-snow sky, who stood at the window of the moving train."

APPLES IN MUNICH

In writing his previous books, Zusak drew upon his own experiences as a Sydneysider to add authentic details to the story. To write a novel set in wartime Germany, Zusak relied on his memories of his parents' stories. He once said that his own childhood proved to be the best research for the book. Zusak's favorite character in the novel is Rudy Steiner, a young German boy with "lemon-colored hair," who idolizes the African American track star Jesse Owens, the gold medalist at the 1936 Berlin Olympics. Rudy blackens his face with charcoal to look like his hero and runs on a local athletic field. This character has some things in common with the author's

American athlete James Cleveland "Jesse" Owens's record-setting performances at the 1936 Olympic Games in Berlin won him four gold medals and demolished Adolf Hitler's myth of Aryan superiority.

father. Rudy hates the Hitler Youth meetings—just as Zusak's father, Helmut, did when he was a boy in Vienna—and decides to stop attending them. Like Helmet, Rudy is selected to attend a special school for Nazis, but his father refuses to let him go and is sent to war as a punishment.

LIVING HISTORY

In 1933, just outside the city of Munich on the grounds of a former ammunition factory, the Nazis built Dachau (pronounced DOCK-cow), the first German concentration camp. Between 1933 and 1945, more than two hundred thousand prisoners from thirty countries were held captive there, forced to work, starved, beaten, and tortured. Many thousands died there. On April 29, 1945, American troops liberated the survivors. This monument to human cruelty now serves as a memorial site and museum.

By the end of World War II, Munich—birthplace of the Nazi Party—had been reduced to rubble. But before the city and its historic buildings were demolished by Allied bombs, the Nazis systematically photographed all of Munich's architecture. When the time came to rebuild the city, its citizens had the choice of either building a new and modern city center or restoring Munich to the way it was before the

Zusak says that 5 percent of the novel is true and the remaining 95 percent is fiction, but to succeed, the story has to ring true. According to Zusak, it is the small details that make a story believable to a reader. For instance, if he wrote that a certain type of apple was ripe in southern

war. They voted to restore it. Today, more than sixty years later, much of the original city has been rebuilt, with the help of those images.

Soldiers and a military band march on New Year's Day, 1939, at the House of German Art in Munich. A tall banner displays the swastika, symbol of the Nazi Party.

Germany during a particular month, he wanted to be certain that was accurate. After he finished the book, Zusak traveled to Munich to make sure he had the details right. He enjoyed visiting the city, even though he felt embarrassed speaking such clumsy German. He walked around the places where his novel was set and saw the river into which he had imagined Rudy jumping. On that spot, he took a coin and scratched Rudy's and Liesel's names into a tree. During the trip, he told *BookPage*, "I did interviews and researched until I couldn't stand it anymore. Research doesn't come naturally to me—in the end, I'm dying to write the story."

THE RUNAWAY SUCCESS OF *THE BOOK THIEF*

CHAPTER SIX

When Zusak first sat down to write *The Book Thief*, he didn't think about whether he was writing a kids' story or one for adults. He just wanted to write a book that would be somebody's favorite. Nonetheless, when he finished the novel, he worried that it would be his least successful one. As Hollywood.com reports, he pictured one reader telling another, "This book is about the Holocaust. It's narrated by Death, there is a high body count, and it's 580 pages long. You'll love it!" He couldn't imagine that a story like that was going to sell. Believing that *The Book Thief* wouldn't succeed actually freed him as a writer. He could write the book that

57

he wanted to write, without having to worry about pleasing a particular audience.

However, booksellers prefer to pigeonhole books and market them to specific age groups or demographics. *The Book Thief* features a ten-year-old protagonist, but it covers some very dark subject matter. This complex story makes demands on its readers. Zusak's publishers in Australia and the United States each chose to market *The Book Thief*

One million free books are given away each year on World Book Night. On April 23, 2012, readers in Denver, Colorado, received copies of *The Book Thief* and other selected works.

to a different audience. In Australia, the novel was published as an adult novel. In the United States, it was marketed as a young adult novel. Zusak wasn't too concerned with the distinctions between adult and young adult literature; he was just glad that the book ended up "in the hands of the right people."

A CRITICAL SUCCESS

Some of those people were the book's publishers. Joan DeMayo, sales director for Random House Children's books, toted Zusak's hefty manuscript along with her to read on a business flight with some of her colleagues. By the time they landed, she knew they had something extraordinary. The company had originally planned to print ten thousand to fifteen thousand copies of the book, but that estimate was quickly revised.

The Book Thief was published in spring 2006. By this point in his writing career, as the author of *The Messenger* and other novels, Zusak had begun to be known beyond his home base of Australia. His new book was reviewed in all the major periodicals. This story about the power of words to destroy and to comfort received warm praise and earned starred reviews in top publications such as *Publishers Weekly, Kirkus Reviews, School Library Journal*, and the *Horn Book Magazine*. The *Wall Street Journal* called it "the most highly anticipated young-adult book in years." Janet

Though he looks like the very picture of success, Zusak has a lot to say about the role that failure has played in his evolution as a writer.

Maslin, a respected book critic for the prestigious *New York Times*, was less enthusiastic than other advance readers, however. Maslin found the book uneven and described it as "a string of anecdotes, tinged with quiet horror."

THE BOOK THIEF: BY THE NUMBERS

How long it took Markus Zusak to write the novel: Three years

Number of times Zusak rewrote the first eighty pages: 150–200 times

Number of pages in the book: 580

Copies of books sold, as of January 2014: More than eight million

Number of languages into which the novel has been translated: Over forty

Number of major awards *The Book Thief* has won: Six

Weeks spent on the *New York Times* best seller list, as of April 2014: 375

TOP OF THE LIST

Despite Maslin's reservations, *The Book Thief* would soon make itself at home on the *New York Times* best seller list. The novel would eventually spend eight years on that list, two years longer than the duration of World War II.

Favorable reviews are a great help, but *The Book Thief* eventually rose to the top of the *New York Times* and other best seller lists because of all the readers who bought the book, loved it, and recommended it to their friends. Word of mouth and online reader reviews have helped drive sales. Since its publication in 2006, sales of *The Book Thief* have

The incredible worldwide success of *The Book Thief* brings fans of all ages and backgrounds to Zusak's book signings, where he takes center stage and captivates attentive audiences.

continued to rise steadily—an unusual phenomenon in the book-selling business. By December 2011, more than two million copies of the book had been sold. As of January 2014, that number had quadrupled. Despite the different audiences to whom the book was marketed, the novel continues to appeal to readers of all ages around the world.

HONORS FOR A THIEF

At the beginning of the novel, Death tells the reader, "It's just a small story, really, about, amongst other things: a girl, some words, an accordionist, some fanatical Germans, a Jewish fist-fighter, and quite a lot of thievery." In 2006, *The Book Thief* won the first of many awards, including the Commonwealth Writers' Prize for Best Book, the *School Library Journal* Best Book of the Year, the Daniel Elliott Peace Award, and *Publishers Weekly*'s Best Children's Book. The following year, it was named a 2007 Michael L. Printz Award Honor Book and Book Sense Book of the Year. Zusak's "small story" was attracting an incredible amount of attention.

ONE BOOK, ONE CITY

For fall 2012, One Book, One Chicago selected *The Book Thief* as the novel that the citizens of the Windy City would all be reading and

A 2012 production of *The Book Thief* at Chicago's legendary Steppenwolf Theatre brought Zusak's novel to the stage as part of a citywide initiative to stop youth violence and intolerance.

discussing. Being chosen for one of these programs is clearly a great honor, not to mention a major boost for book sales. The program involves a series of different events involving libraries, teachers, and schools; high school students; and the general public. As part of One Book, One Chicago, the Steppenwolf Theatre Company produced a stage adaptation of the novel, bringing

Zusak's characters to life onstage. Among other honors, *The Book Thief* was the only book featured on both the U.S. and the U.K. World Book Night Lists in 2012.

THE POWER OF WORDS

A book can have a ripple effect within a community and in the larger culture, once again proving the power of words to bring about change. Zusak has told a story that readers have taken to heart, in the truest sense of the expression. Liesel's courage has inspired courage in others. Teachers have used *The Book Thief* in literature and history classes as a teaching tool against youth violence and to spark discussions about personal responsibility. Zusak set out to write a novel that would satisfy his own ambitions as a writer, but *The Book Thief* has taken on a life of its own.

SEVEN

CHAPTER

COURAGE BEYOND WORDS: THE MAKING OF *THE BOOK THIEF* MOVIE

Since the advent of film, moviemakers have turned to books as a vehicle for story-telling. Approximately one-third of all films made have been adapted from novels. Best-selling books such as *The Hunger Games* and the Harry Potter series have the potential to draw huge audiences and make a pile of money. The film adaptations of these books have broken records at the box office. Buying the film rights to a popular book gives a filmmaker access to a ready-made, well-developed story and compelling characters. In 2013, five of nine films nominated for Best Picture at the Academy Awards were based on books, including that year's winner, *Argo*.

PAYING FOR THE COUCH

In 2006, the year *The Book Thief* was published in the United States, Markus Zusak sold the movie rights to his novel. At the time, he assumed that the book's only shot at success would be if it was made into a film, but he never expected that to happen. He and his wife had just spent more than they could afford on a new couch, and selling the book rights would help to replenish their checking account.

When seven years went by with no further developments, Zusak figured that a *Book Thief* movie was dead in the water. After all, many novels optioned for films never make it into production. He hadn't factored in the determination of Karen Rosenfelt, however. Rosenfelt, who produced the films based on Stephenie Meyers's *Twilight* series, was passionate about bringing *The Book Thief* to the screen.

A RISKY BUSINESS

Adapting a well-loved book for the screen can be risky. Literature and film are two very different mediums, and each relies on different tools and methods

Producer Karen Rosenfelt, who was passionate about bringing *The Book Thief* to the screen, attends a showing of the film at the Holocaust Memorial Museum in Washington, D.C.

to tell a story. Readers who love a book often feel fiercely protective of it; the characters have come to life in their imaginations, and often the actors chosen for the parts can't measure up. Readers don't want to see the story significantly altered onscreen, but film adaptations sometimes fail because they are too faithful to the original work. Some best-selling books that have flopped on film are *Water for Elephants*, *The Time Traveler's Wife*, and *The Great Gatsby*. When he

10 FUN FACTS ABOUT THE AUTHOR

1. Zusak's favorite historical figure is Michelangelo.

2. If he could be anyone else, he would be his brother because he has a much more relaxed attitude about life.

3. If he could choose a fictional character to be his friend, it would either be Sam-I-Am from Dr. Seuss's *Green Eggs and Ham* or Yossarian from Joseph Heller's *Catch-22*.

4. Thirteen is his favorite number.

5. His favorite movies are *Amélie*, *Run Lola Run*, and *The Big Lebowski*.

6. He has two dogs, both of whom he adopted from the pound. Archer is white, and Reuben is a brindle that sits under Zusak's desk as he writes.

7. Zusak is one of Australia's most successful authors.

8. If he could save just one book from a fire it would be *To Kill a Mockingbird*. Because Harper Lee's novel is such a widely loved book, Zusak worries that everyone would assume someone else would save it, and it might be left behind to burn.

9. He is such a nonconfrontational person that he doesn't even like to honk the horn in his car.

10. He doesn't consider himself interesting enough to be the subject of a biography.

learned that the film version of *The Book Thief* was being made, Zusak joked that if people didn't like the movie, they would say the book was better—and he could take comfort in that.

THE ART OF ADAPTATION

Sometimes the author of a book will be hired to adapt it into a screenplay. William Goldman, author of *The Princess Bride*, had great success adapting this and other novels for the screen. Peter Hedges, author of one of Zusak's favorite books, *What's Eating Gilbert Grape* (1991), wrote the screenplay for the 1993 film of the same name. However, not every novelist wants to be a screenwriter or anything other than an author. As Zusak remarked to the *Guardian*, as an author, "the set costs nothing and the actors cost nothing and I'm the director." After finishing *The Book Thief*, Zusak didn't feel up to the task of breaking it into pieces to write a screenplay. He preferred to hand the responsibility over to screenwriter Michael Petroni, whose job it was to transform Zusak's 580-page book into a 120-page script.

FINDING THE GIRL

Eventually, most of the principal roles in the film had been cast. The Australian actor Geoffrey Rush, an Oscar winner (*Shine, The King's Speech*), would play Hans Hubermann, Liesel's accordion-playing foster father. The English actress Emily Watson (*Breaking the Waves*, *Anna Karenina*) would be his wife, Rosa. A thirteen-year-old German actor named Nico Liersch was signed to play Liesel's friend, Rudy Steiner. The role of Max Vandenburg, the Jewish man the Hubermanns hide in their cellar, went to American actor Ben Schnetzer, in his first major role. But the film's producers still hadn't managed to cast the ten-year-old protagonist,

A scene from the movie version of *The Book Thief*, featuring young actors Sophie Nélisse (Liesel) and Nico Liersch (Rudy). Costume and set designers carefully researched period details to ensure the film's visual authenticity.

Liesel, who would have to age seven years in the course of the film. Thousands of actresses auditioned for the role, but no one seemed to combine the qualities of innocence and sheer nerve that the producers were seeking.

Zusak and his wife attended a screening of *Monsieur Lazhar*, a 2011 film about the suicide of a teacher. The movie features the young Canadian actress Sophie Nélisse in her very first screen role. According to the *Guardian*, as they watched her performance, Zusak turned to his wife, Dominika, and said, "That girl would be great in the part of Liesel." At his wife's urging, Zusak mentioned Nélisse's name to the film's producers, and they asked the actress to audition. Zusak delights in the fact "that it took the writer of the novel to find the girl to play the main part."

Nélisse, who was thirteen when the movie was filmed, is a trained gymnast with Olympic aspirations. She almost skipped the audition for the film because she didn't want to miss her training sessions. When they were filming the movie in Berlin, Nélisse decided to get into the role of Liesel and steal some books from a local shop. She figured if she got caught, she would explain that she was just getting into character. She wasn't caught, but of course, a week later, her mother went back to the shop and paid for the books.

NAILING THE DETAILS

After Zusak wrote *The Book Thief*, he traveled to Munich to research the historical setting of his novel. To recreate the world of Nazi Germany during 1939, the film's producers knew they needed to hire a director with an eye for historical accuracy. The Emmy-Award-winning director Brian Percival, whose previous credits included episodes of the television series *Downton Abbey*, seemed a perfect choice.

Zusak joined other *Book Thief* VIPs, including director Brian Percival (*second from right*) and actors Geoffrey Rush (*center*) and Sophie Nélisse (*third from right*), at a screening held at the U.S. Holocaust Memorial Museum.

When his agent sent him the script, Percival stayed up late reading it, even though he had an early shoot the next morning. He was captivated by the story: "I had never read anything in my life that touched me in so many different ways."

Constructed on a sound stage in Berlin, the sets showed impressive attention to detail. Buildings were aged with peeling paint, and fake snow on the ground was laced with streaks of dirt. Zusak had never been on a film set before. It was an incredible experience for him to see his creation brought to life and to walk down Molching's main street, a life-sized replica built for the film. To get the look of the period just right, Oscar-winning costume designer Anna B. Sheppard pored over thousands of mid-twentieth-century photographs of German civilians, adults and children.

NEVER FORGET

The film's producers also expressed hope that *The Book Thief* would introduce the younger viewing audience to a historical period of which they seemed to have limited knowledge. Before appearing in the film, even the younger actors in the movie had only a sketchy understanding of the events that took place in Germany during World War II.

The idea for *The Book Thief* originated in Markus Zusak's childhood kitchen, where his parents' memories of that terrible war became seared in their son's imagination. By a wonderful coincidence, the first scenes of the movie were shot in the kitchen, the heart of the home.

HOW TO LET GO

Ultimately, Zusak considers the film and his book to be two separate entities. To explain this feeling, he drew on an analogy from his own life: "Like brothers, they might look the same at times, and sound it…. But they go their own ways," he wrote in an article published in the *Sydney Morning Herald*. This recognition enabled him to relax and accept the process of making the movie and to trust the director and actors to realize their own vision of the story. After all, as Zusak said, "[T]he film changes things for its own sake, but it can never change the book itself. The book will always remain."

MIXED REVIEWS

Twentieth Century Fox's screen adaptation of *The Book Thief* premiered on November 8, 2013. The poster advertising the film showed an image of Liesel framed by flames and the tagline: "Courage beyond

The promotional poster for *The Book Thief*, featuring Sophie Nélisse as Liesel Meminger. The heroine of the film was the last major role cast for the production.

words." After seeing the film, Zusak's brother kidded that now he didn't have to read the book.

Despite the best efforts of everyone involved with the production, reviews were mixed. The critic in the *New York Times* was especially savage, dismissing the movie as "a shameless piece of Oscar-seeking Holocaust kitsch." Audiences liked the movie considerably more than critics, but the overall consensus was that Zusak's book was far better than the film. As Moira Macdonald wrote in the *Seattle Times*, "This film's audience might be happier at home, curled up with a book. *The Book Thief*, perhaps."

EIGHT

TURNING THE PAGE: *BRIDGE OF CLAY*

On book-signing tours to promote *The Book Thief*, people often asked Zusak what he had planned for his next project. He seemed to have a pretty clear idea and answered without hesitation. In 2008, he told the *Guardian*, "I'm writing a book called *Bridge of Clay*—about a boy building a bridge and wanting it to be perfect. He wants to achieve greatness with this bridge, and the question is whether it will survive when the river floods. That's all I can say about it for now—not out of secrecy, but you just don't know what direction a book is going to take, no matter how well you've planned."

Zusak has been planning *Bridge of Clay* for more than a decade. He believed it would be his breakthrough novel, until

Expectations are high for the yet-to-be-completed *Bridge of Clay*, a coming-of-age story that Zusak has been working on since he finished writing his best seller.

he wrote *The Book Thief*. In interviews, the author sometimes expresses concern that he might not have another book inside him that can measure up to what he accomplished with *The Book Thief*. "It's the first time I've been really worried," Zusak has said, according to SeattlePI.com. "It's the first time I've written a book and thought, 'Can I do a better book?' I don't know if I can." Originally scheduled for publication by Doubleday in fall 2011, more than three years later, *Bridge of Clay* was still delayed.

THE IMPATIENCE OF FANS

When you search online for Zusak's next novel, you will find *Bridge of Clay* listed. You'll see that it is even longer than *The Book Thief*, running to 592 pages. You'll see on the Goodreads website that forty-four online reviewers have given the book 4.12 stars out of a possible five, which is a tad premature, since the book hasn't even been completed yet. And when you scroll down to the comments, you'll see that the online community has plenty to say about the fact that Zusak's next novel has been held up. Often typed in all capital letters, with multiple question marks and exclamation points, comments range from despairing, to furious, to adoring, to sympathetic. Clearly, a large and devoted audience is dying to read whatever Markus Zusak comes up with next.

Perhaps to reassure impatient fans that he is making progress on *Bridge of Clay*, Zusak has posted images of the rough notes from his work and chapter outlines on his Facebook page. He has also shared the first sentence of the novel: "The Murderer arrived at six o'clock, and in the history of all murderers everywhere, this one was surely the most pitiful, at least in terms of appearance."

THE BOOK AFTER
THE BEST SELLER

Many authors say the second book is the hardest one to write. When a novel makes a big splash, it raises the bar very high for the next one. Many writers who have enjoyed dazzling debuts have struggled mightily with the book that followed. Zadie Smith's best-selling novel *White Teeth* (2001) was followed by *The Autograph Man* (2003), which disappointed critics and readers alike. Michael Chabon's *The Mysteries of Pittsburgh* (1988) earned rave reviews and sold extremely well. Chabon's second effort, a fifteen-hundred-page behemoth called *The Fountain*, finally defeated its author and wound up abandoned in a drawer.

Imagine how J. K. Rowling felt when she sat down to write the book that would follow on the heels of the Harry Potter series. Talk about a tough act to follow! That might be why Rowling chose to write a realistic book for adults (*The Casual Vacancy*, 2012), and to follow that with a crime novel titled *The Cuckoo's Calling* (2013), published under the pseudonym Robert Galbraith.

LIFE AFTER SUCCESS

Zusak and his family still live in the southern suburbs of Sydney. Their house backs up to a national park, so they see plenty of wildlife—kookaburras and snakes

Zusak at the Simon Wiesenthal Center's Museum of Tolerance in Los Angeles, a multimedia institution that challenges visitors to confront all forms of discrimination and prejudice in today's world.

and the occasional kangaroo. Zusak's wife, Dominika, works in the personnel department of a supermarket. He is grateful that he didn't marry another writer, since that might make for a challenging coexistence. Writers usually need long stretches of solitude. Zusak works in a quiet room that overlooks the aromatic gray-green leaves of a eucalyptus tree, called a gum tree in Australia, with a sleeping dog at his feet.

NEXT, PLEASE

The Book Thief secured Zusak's future as a writer: he will never again have to worry about supporting himself with his art. However, success comes with plenty of distractions to interrupt a writer's concentration and intrude on his solitude. Time will tell whether Markus Zusak ever manages to build his *Bridge of Clay*. Perhaps he will end up setting this project aside and turning his hand to something else. What's certain is that this author will keep showing up at his desk, day after day, unafraid of failure, ready to risk it all.

ON MARKUS ZUSAK

Full name: Markus Frank Zusak

Birthplace: Sydney, New South Wales, Australia

Birth date: June 23, 1975

Birth order: Youngest of four children

Family heritage: German and Austrian

Current residence: Sydney, New South Wales, Australia

High school attended: Engadine High School

College attended: University of New South Wales, for a teaching degree

First published work: *The Underdog* (novel, 1999)

Early work experience: Painting houses

First paying jobs: High school English teacher, janitor

Marital status: Married to Dominika (Mika) Zusak

Children: Two, a boy and a girl

Hobbies: Surfing, soccer

Pets: Two rescue dogs, Reuben and Archer, and two cats, Bijoux and Brutus

Quotes by Markus Zusak:

"Every time you find something that doesn't work, you're a step closer to what does work."

"I try hard and aim big. People can hate or love my books, but they can never accuse me of not trying."

"I like the idea that every page in every book can have a gem on it. It's probably what I love most about writing—that words can be used in a way that's like a child playing in a sandpit, rearranging things, swapping them around. They're the best moments in a day of writing—when an image appears that you didn't know would be there when you started work in the morning."

"Failure has been my best friend as a writer. It tests you, to see if you have what it takes to see it through."

"I like to tell students, 'I didn't burst on to the literary scene.' I'm never good at things at the beginning. I was terrible at the start. I need to work and work."

ON MARKUS ZUSAK'S WORKS

The Underdog (1999)

Plot summary: Cameron and his older, cooler brother Ruben, siblings from a working-class Australian family, dream up plenty of half-baked schemes in this introductory volume in the Wolfe Brothers trilogy.

Fighting Ruben Wolfe (2000)

Plot summary: In this sequel to *The Underdog*, the Wolfe brothers sign on with a local boxing promoter to face each other in illegal bouts, hoping to raise money for the family after their father loses his job.

Awards received:

2001 Honour Book, CBCA Children's Book of the Year Award, Older Readers (AUS)

2001 Shortlisted for New South Wales Premier's Literary Awards: Ethel Turner Prize for Young People's Literature (AUS)

When Dogs Cry (2001) (U.S. title: *Getting the Girl*)

Plot summary: In the final volume in the Wolfe brothers trilogy, life gets very complicated for younger brother Cameron Wolfe when he falls for his brother Ruben's ex-girlfriend.

Awards received:

2002 Honour Book, CBCA Children's Book of the
Year Award, Older Readers (AUS)

The Messenger (2002) (U.S. title: *I Am the Messenger*)

Plot summary: Down-on-his-luck cab driver Ed
Kennedy becomes an unlikely hero when he
accidentally foils a bank robbery. Shortly after, he
receives in the mail the first of a series of playing
cards inscribed with cryptic messages, directing
him to complete a sequence of mysterious tasks.

Awards received:

2003 New South Wales Premier's Literary Awards: Ethel
Turner Prize for Young People's Literature (AUS)

2003 Children's Book Council of Australia: Book of
the Year Award (AUS)

2005 *Publishers Weekly* Best Books of the Year for
Children

2006 Michael L. Printz Award Honor Book (USA)

2006 Bulletin Blue Ribbon Book (USA)

2007 Deutscher Jugendliteraturpreis (Germany)

The Book Thief (2005)

Plot summary: Narrated by Death, this novel tells the
story of ten-year-old foster child Liesel
Meminger, who grows up in Nazi Germany and
discovers, during the escalation of World War II,
the power of words to bring about both destruction and salvation.

Awards received:

2006 Commonwealth Writers' Prize for Best Book

2006 Daniel Elliott Peace Award

2007 Michael L. Printz Award Honor Book (USA)

2008 IBBY: Ena Noel Award (AUS)

2009 Deutscher Jugendliteraturpreis (Germany)

Adapted for film: *The Book Thief* (Twentieth Century Fox, 2014)

Total copies sold as of January 2014: More than eight million

Number of translations: Forty

Number of weeks on the *New York Times* **best setller list as of April 2014:** 375

Underdogs **(2011),** Omnibus edition of the Wolfe brothers trilogy

THE UNDERDOG

"Zusak's popularity is well-deserved. He writes emo-
tionally engaging stories with understated
humor and a bittersweet style that refuses to
play by straightforward grammatical rules. His
earliest published works share many of the
same stylistic hallmarks and themes of belong-
ing and survival." —*Los Angeles Times*

FIGHTING RUBEN WOLFE

"In earthy, working-class dialect, Australian novelist
Zusak offers a lot of sports action as well as a
sensitive inspection of sibling relationships and
family pride." —*Publishers Weekly*

WHEN DOGS CRY/
GETTING THE GIRL

"Zusak uses simple but poetically poignant language
to convey Cam's inner teenage turmoil, confu-
sion, and heartache. This highly recommended
novel is a sad, funny, loving, and ultimately
heartwarming coming-of-age story."
—*Voice of Youth Advocates*

THE MESSENGER/
I AM THE MESSENGER

"Zusak's characters, styling, and conversations are
believably unpretentious, well conceived, and
appropriately raw. Together, these key elements

fuse into an enigmatically dark, almost film-noir atmosphere where unknowingly lost Ed Kennedy stumbles onto a mystery—or series of mysteries—that could very well make or break his life."
—Hillias J. Martin, New York Public Library

THE BOOK THIEF

"Unsettling, thought-provoking, life-affirming, triumphant and tragic, this is a novel of breathtaking scope, masterfully told. It is an important piece of work, but also a wonderful page-turner."
—*Guardian*

"*The Book Thief* deserves a place on the same shelf with *The Diary of a Young Girl* by Anne Frank and Elie Wiesel's *Night*. It seems poised to become a classic." —*USA Today*

1975 Markus Frank Zusak is born in Sydney, New South Wales, Australia.

1988 Zusak attends Engadine High School in Sydney. He is an unremarkable student.

1991 When he is sixteen, Zusak decides to write a novel but abandons it after only eight pages.

1992 Zusak enrolls at the University of New South Wales, where he majors in English and history. Zusak eventually earns a teaching degree and returns to his high school to teach literature classes. Meanwhile, he continues to work on his writing and begins sending out manuscripts to publishers. He receives many rejections.

1998 While visiting in Vienna, Zusak gets a 2:20 AM phone call from his father informing him that a publisher has accepted his novel *The Underdog*. During this trip to Europe, he also meets his future wife, Dominika (Mika), a fellow Sydneysider.

1999 *The Underdog* is published in Australia.

2000 *Fighting Ruben Wolfe*, a sequel to *The Underdog*, is published. Zusak's second novel wins a Children's Book Council of Australia (CBCA) Children's Book of the Year Award for Older Readers (AUS). The novel is also short-listed for the New South Wales Premier's Literary Awards Ethel Turner Prize for Young People's Literature.

2001 Zusak publishes *When Dogs Cry*, the third and final book in the Wolfe brothers trilogy. The novel is retitled *Getting the Girl* for publication in the United States (2004).

2002 Zusak publishes *The Messenger*, retitled *I Am the Messenger* for U.S. publication (2006). *When Dogs Cry* is named a 2002 Honour Book, CBCA Children's Book of the Year Award: Older Readers (AUS).

2003 *The Messenger* is named Book of the Year by the Children's Book Council of Australia. The novel also wins the New South Wales Premier's Literary Awards Ethel Turner Prize for Young People's Literature.

2004 Zusak finishes writing his fifth novel, titled *The Book Thief.* Zusak travels to Munich to research the historical details in the manuscript.

2005 *The Book Thief* is published in Australia and issued in the United States the following year. *The Messenger* makes the 2005 list of *Publishers Weekly* Best Books of the Year for Children.

2006 Zusak sells the film rights to *The Book Thief.* Later that year, he wins the SMH Best Young Australian Novelist Award and the Kathleen Mitchell Award for literature (AUS). *The Book Thief* makes the *New York Times* best seller list for young adult fiction, where it will remain for the next eight years. The novel is awarded the Commonwealth Writers' Prize for Best Book and wins the Daniel Elliott Peace Award. The novel is also named a *School Library Journal* Best Book of the Year and a *Publishers Weekly* Best Children's Book. *The Messenger* is named a Bulletin Blue Ribbon Book (USA) and a Michael L. Printz Award Honor Book (USA).

2007 *The Messenger* wins the Deutscher Jugendliteraturpreis (Germany). *The Book Thief* is named a Michael L. Printz Award Honor Book (USA).

2008 *The Book Thief* wins an IBBY: Ena Noel Award (AUS).

2009 Zusak wins the Deutscher Jugendliteraturpreis (Germany) for *The Book Thief.*

2011 The Wolfe brothers trilogy is published in an omnibus edition in the United States.

2012 *The Book Thief* is chosen for One Book, One Chicago, a citywide book discussion club.

2013 Premiere of the Twentieth Century Fox film adaptation of *The Book Thief.*

2014 To date, more than eight million copies of *The Book Thief* have been sold. Zusak wins the Margaret A. Edwards Award (USA) for his significant and lasting contribution to young adult literature. As of May, the novel remains on the *New York Times* best seller list, in second place.

ALLIES The nations who united to fight against Germany during World War II, including Britain, France, the Soviet Union, and the United States.

ANKLE-BITER Australian slang for a small child.

ASIDE Dialogue spoken by a character to the audience but unheard by the other characters in a play. Asides are useful for giving the audience special information about the other characters or the action of the plot.

BEST SELLER A book or other product that sells in very large numbers.

BRINDLE An animal with fur that is gray or brownish with obscure dark streaks.

CONCENTRATION CAMP A place where large numbers of people, especially political prisoners or members of persecuted minorities, are imprisoned, sometimes to provide forced labor or to await mass execution.

DUST JACKET A protective, removable paper cover that wraps around a hardcover book.

FILM RIGHTS The rights purchased from the author of a work that enable a filmmaker to make a movie of it.

FIRST-PERSON NARRATIVE A story told from the point of view of a single observer, referring to him- or herself (the "I").

FOOTBALLER An Australian or British term for what is known in the United States as a soccer player.

GENRE A category of artistic composition, as in literature or music, characterized by similarities in form, style, or subject matter.

HITLER YOUTH An organization founded in 1926, used to educate and train boys in Nazi principles. By 1939, all German males under age seventeen were required to join. By 1941, membership was also required for those over the age of ten.

HOLOCAUST The systematic extermination of eleven million European Jews and other individuals considered undesirable (including homosexuals and people of Roma descent) carried out by Nazi Germany prior to and during World War II.

IMMIGRANT A person who comes to live permanently in a foreign country.

JEW A member of the people and cultural community whose traditional religion is Judaism and who trace their origins through the ancient Hebrew people of Israel to Abraham.

NAZI A member of a German political party that controlled Germany from 1933 to 1945 under Adolf Hitler.

NEW SOUTH WALES A state on Australia's southeast coast where Sydney is the capital city.

NOVEL A long, written story about imaginary characters and events; a literary genre.

NOVELLA A fictional prose narrative that is longer and more complex than a short story, but shorter than a novel.

OMNIBUS A book containing reprints of a number of books.

OZ A slang term for the country of Australia.

PENAL COLONY A remote location, often an island or distant colonial territory, where prisoners are sent to live to separate them from the general population.

PERSONIFY To attribute human qualities to an inanimate object or abstraction.

PROTAGONIST The main character in a novel, film, drama, or other fictional text.

PSEUDONYM An assumed name or alias used by a writer to disguise his or her authorship of a written work.

SADISTIC Deriving pleasure from inflicting pain, suffering, or humiliation on others.

THE SHIRE A local name for the southern suburbs of Sydney, Australia.

SHORTLISTED Put on a list of candidates selected for final consideration.

SIBLING RIVALRY Competition between siblings for the attention, affection, and approval of a parent.

SYDNEYSIDER A citizen of Sydney, Australia.

UNDERDOG A competitor believed to have little chance of winning a fight or a contest.

WORKING CLASS A social group consisting of people who are employed for wages, especially in manual or industrial work.

YOUNG ADULT (YA) A genre of literature traditionally written for readers aged sixteen to twenty-five.

Creative Writers Workshop
Department of Professional Studies and Special
Programs
Emerson College
120 Boylston Street
Boston, MA 02116
(617) 824-8280
Website: http://www.emerson.edu/academics/
professional-studies/programs-high
-school-students
The Creative Writers Workshop, held every summer
at Emerson College, gives rising high school
sophomores, juniors, and seniors the chance to
develop their writing process and create and
present works of fiction, nonfiction, poetry,
screenwriting, and more.

Great Books Summer Program
P.O. Box 743
Fairfield, CT 06824
(866) 480-7323
Website: http://www.greatbookssummer.com
Every summer, the Great Books Summer Program
brings distinguished college professors to the
campuses of Amherst, Oxford, and Stanford to
teach middle school and high school students
to engage with literature. Students read and
think critically about seminal works and hone
their writing skills with peer and mentor support.

Montreal Holocaust Memorial Centre
5151, Chemin de la Côte-Sainte-Catherine

(Cummings House)
Montréal, QC H3W 1M6
Canada
(514) 345-2605
Website: http://www.mhmc.ca
Through its exhibits and collections, the Montreal
    Holocaust Memorial Centre seeks to educate
    the public about the Holocaust, bringing
    special attention to the universal perils of
    anti-Semitism, racism, hate, and indifference.

National Museum of Australia
GPO Box 1901
Canberra, ACT 2601
Australia
+ 61 2 6208 5000
Website: http://www.nma.gov.au
This social history museum is devoted to the land,
    nation, and people of Australia and educates
    visitors about indigenous histories and cultures
    of European settlement.

National WWII Museum
945 Magazine Street
New Orleans, LA 70130
(504) 528-1944
Website: http://www.nationalww2museum.org
Founded by author and historian Stephen Ambrose,
    this museum tells the story of the American
    experience in World War II.

NSW Migration Heritage Centre
P.O. Box K346
Haymarket, NSW 1238
Australia
+61 2 9217 0625
Website: http://www.migrationheritage.nsw.gov.au
The centre is a virtual (online) immigration museum. The
        website is a gateway to learn about the rich and
        varied migration heritage of New South Wales
        through community collections, family belongings,
        people's memories, and special places.

PEN/Faulkner Foundation
201 East Capitol Street SE
Washington, DC 20003
(202) 898-9063
Website: http://www.penfaulkner.org
In addition to administering its namesake award, the
        Pen/Faulkner Foundation encourages readers of
        all ages to connect to writing through its various
        events and education initiatives. Its Writers in
        Schools program is a literary outreach service,
        bringing authors to visit local D.C. high schools
        and discuss both writing and literature.

Read.gov: One Book Programs
Library of Congress
101 Independence Avenue SE
Washington, DC 20540
(202) 707-5000
Website: http://www.read.gov

A place to search for One Book programs in different U.S. states, or to find resources for starting one's own One Book project, this site also provides information about book fairs and storytelling festivals around the United States.

Sydney Jewish Museum
148 Darlinghurst Road
Darlinghurst, NSW 2010
Australia
+ 61 2 9360 7999
Website: http://www.sydneyjewishmuseum.com.au
At the Sydney Jewish Museum, visitors can gain insight into the events of the Holocaust by meeting people who were involved. The museum also teaches about Jewish history and explores Jewish life in Australia.

Teen Ink
P.O. Box 30
Newton, MA 02461
(617) 964-6800
Website: http://www.teenink.com
Teen Ink is a monthly print magazine, Web site, and book series all written by teens, for teens.

Teen Writers Club (Australia)
Website: http://www.teenwrite.webs.com
The Teen Writers Club is an Australian site for teen writers around the world, with articles, opportunities to post their work, discuss and improve their writing, and more.

United States Holocaust Memorial Museum
100 Raoul Wallenberg Place SW
Washington, DC 20024
(202) 488-0400
Website: http://www.ushmm.org
The United States Holocaust Memorial Museum
inspires citizens and leaders worldwide to learn
from the Holocaust and confront hatred, pre-
vent genocide, and promote human dignity.

Young Writers of Canada
Poetry Institute of Canada and Young Writers
P.O. Box 44169-RPO Gorge
Victoria, BC V9A 7K1
Canada
(250) 519-0446
Website: http://www.youngwritersofcanada.ca
Now in its twentieth year, the Young Writers division of
Young Writers of Canada holds annual poetry/
short story contests for writers ages seven to
eighteen. Contests are free to enter, and winning
entries are publishing in an anthology.

WEBSITES

Because of the changing nature of Internet links,
Rosen Publishing has developed an online list of
websites related to the subject of this book. This
site is updated regularly. Please use this link to
access the list:

http://www.rosenlinks.com/AAA/Zusak

FOR FURTHER READING

Anflick, Charles. *Resistance: Teen Partisans and Resisters Who Fought Nazi Tyranny*. New York, NY: Rosen Publishing, 1999.

Atwood, Kathryn J. *Women Heroes of World War II*. Chicago, IL: Chicago Review Press, 2013.

Baker, Tim. *Australia's Century of Surf*. North Sydney, NSW, Australia: Random House Australia, 2014.

Bartoletti, Susan Campbell. *Hitler Youth: Growing Up in Hitler's Shadow*. New York, NY: Scholastic Inc., 2005.

Buchignani, Walter. *Tell No One Who You Are: The Hidden Childhood of Régine Miller*. Toronto, ON, Canada: Tundra, 2008.

Castagna, Felicity. *The Incredible Here and Now*. Artarmon, NSW, Australia: Giramondo Publishing, 2013.

DK Publishing. *Munich and the Bavarian Alps*. New York, NY: DK Publishing, 2014.

Dowswell, Paul. *Auslander*. London, England: Bloomsbury Publishing PLC, 2010.

Edmondson, Jacqueline. *Jesse Owens: A Biography*. Westport, CT: Greenwood, 2007.

Ephron, Hallie. *The Everything Guide to Writing Your First Novel*. Avon, MA: Adams Media Corporation, 2010.

Gleeson-White, Jane. *Australian Classics: 50 Great Writers and Their Celebrated Works*. Crows Nest, NSW: Allen & Unwin, 2011.

Hamen, Susan E. *Australia*. Minneapolis, MN: ABDO Publishing Company, 2013.

Hilton, Christopher. *Hitler's Olympics*. Charleston, NC: The History Press, 2011.

Holliday, Laurel. *Children in the Holocaust and World War II: Their Secret Diaries*. New York, NY: Washington Square Press, 1996.

Hoskins, Ian. *Sydney Harbour: A History*. Sydney, NSW, Australia: UNSW Press, 2011.

Jarratt, Phil. *Australia's Hottest 100 Surfing Legends*. New York, NY: Rizzoli, 2012.

Karskens, Grace. *The Colony: A History of Early Sydney*. Crows Nest, NSW, Australia: Allen & Unwin, 2011.

Lemmin-Woolfrey, Ulrike. *Sydney & the Great Barrier Reef*. New York, NY: Avalon Travel Publishing, 2014.

Miller, John. *Australia's Writers and Poets*. Wollombi, NSW, Australia: Exisle Publishing, 2011.

Rappaport, Doreen. *Beyond Courage: The Untold Story of Jewish Resistance During the Holocaust*. Somerville, MA: Candlewick Press, 2012.

Sharenow, Robert. *The Berlin Boxing Club*. New York, NY: HarperCollins, 2011.

West, Barbara A. *A Brief History of Australia*. New York, NY: Facts On File, 2010.

Winchester, Elizabeth Siris. *Sisters and Brothers*. New York, NY: Scholastic, 2008.

Wright, Heather. *Writing Fiction: A Hands-on Guide for Teens*. North Charleston, SC: CreateSpace Publishing, 2014.

Barta, Preston. "Interview: Markus Zusak, Geoffrey Rush and Cast on 'The Book Thief.'" November 26, 2013. Retrieved April 18, 2014 (http://ntdaily.com/interview-markus-zuzak-geoffrey-rush-cast-on-the-book-thief).

Blauvelt, Christian. "'The Book Thief' First Look: How Markus Zusak's Novel Became a Likely Oscar Contender." Hollywood.com, September 20, 2013. Retrieved April 19, 2014 (http://www.hollywood.com/news/movies/55030324/the-book-thief-movie-markus-zusak-geoffrey-rush).

Carpenter, Susan. "Not Just for Kids: 'UnderDogs' by Markus Zusak." Review of *UnderDogs* by Markus Zusak, *Los Angeles Times*, August 14, 2011. Retrieved April 5, 2014 (http://articles.latimes.com/2011/aug/14/entertainment/la-ca-markus-zusak-20110814).

Catton, Jade. "November 18, 2009 (10:19 p.m.) Comment on 'The Book Thief, Markus Zusak.'" *Reading the End* blog, January 23, 2008. Retrieved April 18, 2014 (http://readingtheend.com/2008/01/23/the-book-thief-markus-zusak).

Charles, Ron, "'Book Thief' Author Markus Zusak Remembers Humble Beginnings," *Washington Post* style blog, February 23, 2013. Retrieved April 5, 2014 (http://www.washingtonpost.com/blogs/style-blog/wp/2013/02/23/book-thief-author-markus-zusak-remembers-humble-beginnings).

Chicago Public Library."*The Book Thief*: One Book, One Chicago." Fall 2012. Retrieved April 15, 2014

(http://www.chipublib.org/the-book
-thief-one-book-one-chicago-fall-2012).

Children's Department. "10 Questions with Markus
Zusak." Politics and Prose Bookstore and Modern
Times Coffeehouse. Retrieved April 12, 2014
(http://www.politics-prose.com/10-questions/10
-questions-markus-zusak-0).

Clement, Jessica. "The Book Thief Author Markus
Zusak Lets Go of Novel and Allows Filmmakers to
Follow Vision." *Wentworth Courier*, January 13,
2014. Retrieved April 16, 2014 (http://www
.dailytelegraph.com.au/newslocal/city-east/the
-book-thief-author-markus-zusak-lets-go-of-novel
-and-allows-filmmakers-to-follow-vision/story
-fngr8h22-1226799158179).

Farrey, Brian. "Author Interview." Teenreads.com, April
2006. Retrieved April 3, 2014 (http://www
.teenreads.com/authors/markus-zusak/news/
interview-040906).

French, Mike. "Interview with Markus Zusak." The View
From Here, March 3, 2009. Retrieved April 5, 2014
(http://www.viewfromheremagazine.com/2009/03/
interview-with-markus-zusak.html).

Goodnow, Cecelia. "Australian Writer Markus Zusak Is
Already a Literary Sensation." SeattlePI.com, April
5, 2006. Retrieved April 20, 2014 (http://www
.seattlepi.com/ae/books/article/Australian-writer
-Markus-Zusak-is-already-a-1200296.php#
page-2).

Holden, Stephen. "A Refuge Found in Pages." *New
York Times*, November 7, 2013. Retrieved April 18,

2014 (http://www.nytimes.com/2013/11/08/
movies/the-book-thief-world-war-ii-tale-with
-geoffrey-rush.html?_r=0).

Kenber, Ben. "Interview with Brian Percival and Markus
Zusak on 'The Book Thief.' Examiner.com,
November 13, 2013. Retrieved on April 18, 2014
(http://www.examiner.com/article/interview-with
-brian-percival-and-markus-zusak-on-the-book
-thief).

Kinson, Sarah. "Markus Zusak." *Guardian*, March 28,
2008. Retrieved April 5, 2014 (http://www
.theguardian.com/books/2008/mar/28/whyiwrite).

Kirkus Reviews. "The Book Thief by Markus Zusak."
Kirkus, May 20, 2010. Retrieved April 17, 2014
(https://www.kirkusreviews.com/book-reviews/
markus-zusak/fighting-ruben-wolfe).

Maslin, Janet. "Stealing to Settle a Score with Life."
New York Times, March 27, 2006. Retrieved April
12, 2014 (http://www.nytimes.com/2006/03/27/
books/27masl.html?8hpib&_r=0).

Miller, Nick. "Novel Ambition." *Sydney Morning Herald*,
November 23, 2013. Retrieved April 12, 2014
(http://www.smh.com.au/entertainment/books/
novel-ambition-20131118-2xpu0.html).

O'Shaughnessy, Gillian. "Markus Zusak, Author of *The
Book Thief*, on Writing and Film Success." 720
ABC Perth, January 17, 2014. Retrieved April 13,
2014 (http://www.abc.net.au/local/stories/2014/
01/17/3927439.htm).

Pauli, Michelle. "Markus Zusak: The Book Thief Film's
Biggest Hurdle Was Death." *Guardian*, February
25, 2014. Retrieved April 6, 2014 (http://www

.theguardian.com/childrens-books-site/2014/
feb/25/book-thief-markus-zusak-interview?INTCM
P=ILCNETTXT3487).

Powell's Books. "Kids' Q&A, Markus Zusak." Retrieved
April 5, 2014 (http://www.powells.com/kidsqa/
zusak.html).

Publishers Weekly. "Children's book review of The Book
Thief, by Markus Zusak." January 30, 2006.
Retrieved April 4, 2014 (http://www
.publishersweekly.com/9780375831003).

Random House. "Markus Zusak Author Bookshelf."
Retrieved April 6, 2014 (http://www.randomhouse.
com/author/59222/markus-zusak).

Young Adult Library Services Association (YALSA).
"Margaret A. Edwards." Retrieved April 22, 2014
(http://www.ala.org/yalsa/Edwards).

Zusak, Markus. The Book Thief. New York, NY: Random
House Children's Books, 2007.

Zusak, Markus. "How I Let Go of The Book Thief."
Sydney Morning Herald, January 4, 2014.
Retrieved April 19, 2014 (http://www.smh.com
.au/entertainment/movies/markus-zusak
-how-i-let-go-of-the-book-thief-20140102-
306he.html).

Zusak, Markus. I Am the Messenger. New York, NY:
Random House Children's Books, 2006.

Zusak, Markus. "Markus Zusak Talks About the Writing
of The Book Thief." Retrieved April 3, 2014 (http://
www.panmacmillan.com.au/resources/MZ
-TheBookThief.pdf).

Zusak, Markus. Underdogs. New York, NY: Arthur A.
Levine, 2011.

INDEX

A

Anthony, Piers, 51
Australian Children's
    Book Award, 35, 40
awards, book, 41–43

B

Book Sense Book of the
    Year, 63
Book Thief, The,
    6, 48–56, 78, 79,
    80, 83
    adaptation into movie,
    67–77
    adaptation into play,
    64–65
    awards won, 63
    effect of, 65
    marketing of,
    58–59, 63
    reviews of, 59–61
    statistics on, 61
    story of, 48–49,
    50–54
    success of, 61–63
Book Thief, The (movie),
    67–77
    actors in, 70–72
    reviews of, 77
Bridge of Clay, 78–79,
    80, 83

C

Chabon, Michael, 81
Children's Book Council of
    Australia, 35, 41
Commonwealth Writers'
    Prize for Best Book, 63

D

Daniel Elliot Peace
    Award, 63
death, personification of, 51
DeMayo, Joan, 59
Deutscher Jugendliterature
    prize, 41
Dirty Job, A, 51
Discworld, 51

E

Edwards, Margaret A., 42
Engadine High School,
    20, 26
Ethel Turner Prize
    for Young People's
    Literature, 35,
    40–41, 43

F

Fighting Ruben Wolfe,
    33–35, 40

film adaptations of books, 66–70

G

Gaiman, Neil, 51
Getting the Girl, 37, 40
Goldman, William, 70
Grug (character), 15
Grug and the Red Apple, 15

H

Harry Potter series, 66, 81
Hedges, Peter, 23, 70
Hemingway, Ernest, 23
Hitler, Adolf, 10, 54
Holocaust, 8, 54, 57, 77
Hunger Games, The, 66

L

Liersch, Nico, 71

M

Masque of the Red Death, The, 51
Messenger, The (*I Am the Messenger*), 38–41, 45, 59
adaptation into play, 41
awards won, 40–41

reviews of, 40
story of, 38–39
Meyers, Stephenie, 67
Michael L. Printz Honor Book Award, 41, 43, 63
Moore, Christopher, 51
Mueller, Ross, 41
Munich, Germany, 10, 54, 56, 73

N

Nazi Party, 10, 54, 73
Nélisse, Sophie, 72

O

On a Pale Horse, 51
One Book, One Chicago, 63–64

P

Percival, Brian, 73–74
Petroni, Michael, 70
Poe, Edgar Allen, 51
Pratchett, Terry, 51
Princess Bride, The, 70
Printz, Michael L., 43
Prior, Ted, 15
Publishers Weekly Best Children's Book, 63

R

Random House, 59
Rosenfelt, Karen, 67
Rowling, J. K., 51, 81
Rush, Geoffrey, 70

S

Sandman, The, 51
Schnetzer, Ben, 71
School Library Journal
    Best Book of the
    Year, 63
Sheppard, Anna B., 74
Smith, Zadie, 81
Steppenwolf Theatre
    Company, 64
Strine, 14, 15
Sydney, Australia,
    9, 12–13, 20,
    21, 81

T

*Tales of Beedle the Bard,
    The*, 51
Turner, Ethel, 43
Twilight, 67

U

Underdog, The, 30, 31

accepted by
    publisher, 32
release of, 32–33
story of, 28,
    30–31, 33
Underdogs trilogy, 22,
    33–37, 45
University of New South
    Wales, 24–25

W

Watson, Emily, 71
*What's Eating Gilbert
    Grape*, 70
*When Dogs Cry (Getting the
    Girl)*, 35–37
World War II, 10, 46–48,
    62, 74
writing, tips for, 22,
    23, 30, 34

Z

Zusak, Dominika, 32, 67,
    72, 83
Zusak, Elizabeth, 10–12,
    14, 23, 46–48, 49, 75
Zusak, Helmut, 12, 13,
    17–19, 23, 54, 75
Zusak, Markus
    awards won, 35
    begins writing, 19, 22, 23,

24, 27
childhood, 9–10, 13–19,
    20–24
in college, 24–25
facts about, 69
popularity, 6, 8, 40,
    59, 80
relationship with
    brother, 10, 14,

20, 22, 31, 32, 45,
    69, 77
and surfing,
    21–22, 30
as teacher, 26–27
wife and children,
    32, 67, 72, 83
writing routine and style,
    30, 34, 45, 49

ABOUT THE AUTHOR

Monique Vescia's first career was in children's book publishing. Now she is a writer with many nonfiction books to her credit. Other authors she has written about include Louis Sachar (*Holes*) and Elizabeth George Speare (*The Witch of Blackbird Pond*). Monique makes her home in Seattle with her husband and their teenage son.

PHOTO CREDITS

Cover, p. 3 Gilbert Carrasquillo/Getty Images; p. 7 Ouzounova/Splash News/Newscom; pp. 10–11 Horace Abrahams/Hulton Archive/Getty Images; p. 12 Klaus Hollitzer/iStock/Thinkstock; pp. 16–17 Andreas Altenburger/Shutterstock.com; pp. 18–19 auremar/Shutterstock.com; p. 21 Jean-Pierre Muller/AFP/Getty Images; p. 25 expose/Shutterstock.com; p. 26 hobbit/Shutterstock.com; pp. 29, 62, 79 Michael Tulberg/Getty Images; pp. 36–37, 44 David Levenson/Getty Images; p. 39 dtsuneo/iStock/Thinkstock; p. 42 Courtesy of the Enoch Pratt Free Library; p. 47 FPG/Archive Photos/Getty Images; p. 53 AFP/Getty Images; p. 55 Hugo Jaeger/Time & Life Pictures/Getty Images; p. 58 RJ Sangosti/The Denver Post/Getty Images; p. 60 Caroline McCredie/Getty Images; p. 64 Kristyna Archer/The New York Times/Redux; pp. 68, 73 Larry French/Getty Images; p. 71 Jules Heath/20th Century Fox/AP Images; p. 76 Rex Features/AP Images; p. 82 Eric Charbonneau/Invision for 20th Century Fox/AP Images; cover, interior pages (book) © www.istockphoto.com/Andrzej Tokarski; cover, interior pages (textured backgrounds) javarman/Shutterstock.com and © iStockphoto.com/HadelProductions.

Designer: Nicole Russo; Editor: Shalini Saxena